The Butchart Gardens®
▪OVER 100 YEARS IN BLOOM▪
NATIONAL HISTORIC SITE OF CANADA

A Family
Legacy

Text by David Clarke
Research by David Clarke, Carmen Moore and Janet Beveridge

Modern scene photography by Bonnie Burton and John Bailey
Design by Laura Lasby

© 2006 The Butchart Gardens Ltd.
All rights reserved

Published by The Butchart Gardens Ltd.
Box 4010, Victoria, BC, Canada, V8X 3X4

The Butchart Gardens and the cement plant at Tod Inlet 1956

The Butchart Gardens is located on Saanich Inlet, an arm of the Pacific Ocean some 13 miles north of Victoria, the provincial capital of British Columbia on Vancouver Island. Influenced by a prevailing westerly flow of marine air, the benevolent climate of the island is spared the harshness of the mainland Canadian winter. This feature of life on Vancouver Island contributes to the number of fine gardens with a huge variety and abundance of trees, shrubs, plants and flowers. The attraction of being able to be outside in the garden all year round may have impressed Jennie and R.P. Butchart when they first came to the island from eastern Canada in 1902.

Robert Pim Butchart

The Butchart family of Grey County, Ontario, can be traced back to the Strathmore area of Scotland about 150 miles north of Edinburgh. Brothers James and Andrew came to Canada from the town of Forfar in the 1820's. The grandson of James, Robert Pim Butchart, was born in Owen Sound, Ontario in 1856, the oldest son of eleven children. He and his brother David inherited the family hardware and ship chandlery business in that thriving lakeshore community on Georgian Bay.

Jennie Butchart

Jennie Foster Kennedy was born in Toronto in 1866. Orphaned early in her life, Jennie was made a 'ward in chancery' with an established lawyer, Sir William Mulock, later to be Canada's Postmaster General, who sent her to live with an aunt at Owen Sound. The environment of Owen Sound apparently suited Jennie and she displayed great talent both as a horsewoman and an artist.

She was awarded a scholarship to study art in Paris. Jennie also obtained a certificate as a chemist which was to assist her later in life. In 1884 she married Robert Butchart and put aside thoughts of pursuing her art scholarship in Europe.

In 1888 R.P. joined with a group proposing to manufacture Portland cement which at that time was imported for use in Canada from English sources. Their venture was unsuccessful owing to a problem with the extremely high temperature necessary in the kilns used to burn the crushed limestone. The firebrick lining the kiln was not able to withstand these temperatures and burned through. The failure of this company did not deter Butchart, who took over the factory, changing its name to the "Owen Sound Portland Cement Company". He travelled to England in 1890 in search of expertise and improved equipment.

While in the county of Kent near Rochester, he noticed a shingle bearing the name "Jas. Butchart: Consulting Engineer". He introduced himself and found that James Butchart held an interest in two cement works nearby, that he knew the business and was willing to assist Robert in his quest. Back in Canada the problem seemed to lie with the temperatures at which the crushed rock was being burned. James Butchart was able to suggest a type of kiln that corrected the fault. So began a long and rewarding friendship between the two distant relatives. Robert Pim Butchart went on to successfully build and operate two factories that manufactured Portland cement at Owen Sound and Lakefield, Ontario. Jennie's value as a chemist in the laboratories of her husband's cement factories conducting product tests and analyses proved to be of great value during those early years of the Canadian Portland cement industry.

In 1902, Robert and Jennie travelled to Tod Inlet on Vancouver Island to assess a limestone deposit as a possible site for a factory to supply cement for projects on the rapidly developing west coast of Canada. More than forty years later Jennie related her recollection of the day when she and Bob arrived by horsedrawn buggy to meet with a Mr. Fernie who was leasing the land close by. As she waited, holding the horses, her husband took a shortcut across the field. Hearing a noise behind him he turned to see a bull rushing at him and he scrambled up a burnt tree stump to escape. A man watching from a window in a nearby cottage came to the door, presumably to get a better view of the proceedings, and Bob called out to him to get the bull away.

Mining limestone in the quarry

The cement plant at Tod Inlet circa 1908

" 'Tain't my bull", said the man and closed the door. Jennie Butchart always hoped that those who came to visit her garden in the years to come would feel more welcome than she and her husband had felt when they came that first time to Tod Inlet. However, they were enchanted with the scenery and the climate, and they arranged for their two daughters, Jennie and Mary, to join them in Victoria. The Butchart family spent their first two summers in a small house on the site of today's residence. For the rest of the year they stayed in the city of Victoria. Later, in 1904, Robert was to write in a letter to one of the directors of the newly founded Vancouver Portland Cement Company,

"Search the world over it would be hard to find a more suitable location for manufacturing cement. Trap rock and lime rock for building are within a stone's throw, running water for concrete and gravel within two miles by scow. There is rock and clay (for manufacturing cement) which can be conveyed by gravity to the crusher - and a pretty, land locked harbour! With coal within 50 miles by water, all we lack is that most important item - a large market!"

As the cement industry flourished on the west coast so did Jennie Butchart's creation of her garden. Her skill as a gardener was entirely self-taught. The weather on Vancouver Island, in extreme contrast to that of Ontario, allowed gardening to be a year round activity which must have encouraged her in her new found enterprise. Her first area of activity was as far away as possible from the industry of the limestone quarry. There, with the rock blasting and drilling creating so much noise and dust, creation of a garden would have been an impossibility. Jennie chose instead the gentle slope down to the sea at Butchart Cove to start her Japanese Garden in 1906.

The entrance to that garden was marked, as it is today, with a red-lacquered torii gate. On either side of this gate two beech trees were planted. These trees, along with several Japanese maples, were the first non-native trees to be introduced to the garden. For the first two or three years Jennie was assisted in her endeavours by Isaburo Kishida, a garden designer from Japan. Her ideas of a Japanese Garden may have clashed somewhat with those of the Japanese expert. As an example of this, a torii gate traditionally stands at the entrance to a Shinto shrine. In addition, Jennie's plans seemed to call for more flowering plants and fewer dry stream and rock areas. As a result, this garden is more a North American impression of a Japanese Garden in line with Jennie's wishes. In the years to come Kishida would be responsible for several more traditional Japanese gardens such as that at Hatley Castle at Royal Roads near Victoria.

In 1909, after five years of excavation, the quarry was abandoned as a source of limestone for the nearby factory. The barren floor and walls of the industrial site created a challenge to Jennie Butchart who by now had worked wonders with the garden she had developed closer to the residence. Encouraged by the enthusiasm of visitors to their home and garden, Jennie decided to landscape and plant the quarry as a sunken garden.

The Sunken Garden begins to take shape circa 1912

In 1908 the Butcharts hired Hugh Lindsay, a gardener from Scotland, who became the first head gardener. The lodge at the end of the exit road leading from the Butcharts gardens was built to accommodate Mr. Lindsay's family when they came out from Scotland to join him. He worked with Jennie Butchart through the initial planning stages of the Sunken Garden until 1913.

She was also supported in her project by her husband who readily supplied manpower for the heavy task of bringing in all the topsoil to create the beds on the bare rock floor. Jennie herself took on the task of planting ivy in cracks and crevices to cover the stark stone walls.

The Sunken Garden circa 1912

This was accomplished using a bosun's chair suspended from the edge of the quarry. As if in a demonstration of her far-sighted approach to the project, a row of Lombardy poplar saplings was planted to hide from view the grey walls and lofty chimney stacks of the Portland cement factory. These trees stand nearly one hundred years later as testament to her resolution to succeed in the task of refurbishment and beautification. Ironically, the factory and all its buildings, apart from one stack that remains today, were demolished in 1993. The art of gardening once again outlasted the brief life of industry!

Bringing in top soil by horse and cart circa 1912

The residence circa 1911

The house in which the Butcharts lived at Tod Inlet was really only suitable as a summer home. When they decided to take up full time residence, alterations and improvements were necessary. Changes were also made to the surroundings. A lawn was laid, stretching from the house to the head of the Japanese Garden. Inside their residence Robert and Jennie made changes to accommodate an increasing number of friends and business associates who came to stay. The well-known Canadian architect, Samuel Maclure, was engaged to remodel and enlarge the Butchart home. A sizeable quantity of lumber was purchased in 1911 and a start was made. A billiard room was added in 1913 at the other side of the residence, as well as a small saltwater swimming pool with aviary, overlooking the tennis court, now the Italian Garden.

The living room circa 1930's

In 1922, the Conservatory was constructed leading off a sitting room, and a private garden for Jennie Butchart alongside the house. To this day this is the only garden area not open to the public. The Butcharts always enjoyed travelling, often taking ocean voyages to Africa, Europe and the Far East. The countless friendships they made overseas resulted in a great number of visitors to Vancouver Island. Their home, named Benvenuto or 'Welcome' in Italian, earned its name in providing gracious hospitality to all their guests.

They also seldom returned from a trip without some new plant with which to improve and enhance their gardens. On his travels R.P. was an enthusiastic keeper of travel diaries, especially with regard to daily expenses and golf scores, both his and Jennie's. During one visit to England in the winter of 1913, over a period of four and a half months, R.P. recorded 84 rounds of golf on a variety of courses in the south of England, together with visits to many stately homes with their magnificent gardens.

The dining room circa 1930s

In the early years many of their acquaintances from Victoria and business associates from the cement industry would meet socially in London to enjoy the theatre and major sporting events.

Mr. and Mrs. Harry Ross and their son, Ian

The Breakfast Room in the residence

In 1917, Jennie, the Butcharts' elder daughter, married Harry Ross, R.P.'s personal assistant in the cement business. Their son Ian was born in 1918. As Mr. and Mrs. Butchart were so often out of the country in the winter months, Harry was responsible for keeping them in touch with events back at the company. When the health of R.P. became frail and necessitated extended stays for treatment at a sanitarium in California, Harry Ross became increasingly important in the management of the cement company.

Visitors were coming to Vancouver Island from all parts of North America to see the Butcharts' garden. Many letters were written expressing appreciation of the work that had been done. The Butcharts would take the time to reply graciously as shown in this letter to a lady in San Francisco:

"Dear Madam,

I appreciate the kind thought which prompted you to write me such a kind and complimentary letter. Coming from one living in your beautiful California makes the compliment doubly appreciated. Mrs. Butchart and I always feel gratified when those who love flowers and things beautiful visit our garden, and go away feeling as you have, that their time has not been wasted. We receive so many nice letters from people who have visited the garden, but whom we have never met, that we feel well repaid for our efforts, chiefly my wife's, for having striven to make the place attractive. Thanking you, and trusting that when you come to Victoria again, we may have the pleasure of meeting you.

Sincerely yours, R.P.B."

Mr. and Mrs. Butchart with a young family friend on a pony

The Butchart grandchildren and their friends enjoyed visits to the gardens - especially in the summer holidays. Croquet hoops and archery targets were regular fixtures on the main lawn. Evidently even pony rides were permitted when there were young visitors to be entertained.

Mrs. Butchart in the Rose Garden

Meconopsis *baileyi*

The Tibetan blue poppy

Meconopsis baileyi has been grown with great success in Jennie Butchart's garden since the mid 1920's. Seed from this attractive plant is still collected and packaged for sale here at The Butchart Gardens. The Himalayan blue poppy first came to Mrs. Butchart as seed from England. Although this charming flower had been brought back as a plant to Europe by a French missionary in the mid 1800's, it was a captain in the British army, on active duty, who collected a specimen of the poppy in 1913 in eastern Tibet and delivered it to the Director of the Royal Botanical Society at Kew Gardens in England. The society named the new arrival Meconopsis baileyi for its discoverer, Frederic Marshman Bailey. Although there was no seed of the plant, Captain Bailey had recorded the location of his discovery quite accurately. This enabled the plant-hunter and seedsman, F. Kingdon-Ward, to locate the poppies in that distant location some ten years later.

He brought back a pound or two of seed and hundreds of plants were raised by members of the Royal Horticultural Society. Ultimately seed was obtained by Jennie Butchart who found that conditions were ideal for its propagation on Vancouver Island. When Captain Bailey visited Jennie Butchart in her garden some years later he was greatly surprised to see his poppy blooming vigorously in her Japanese Garden.

Benvenuto Seed Company

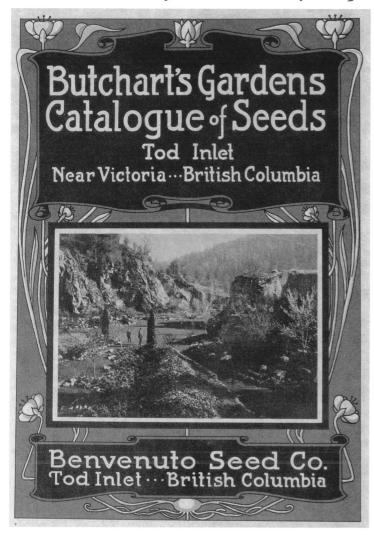

An early seed catalogue

Jennie Butchart

In answer to many requests for seed from the flowers in her garden, Jennie Butchart began to plant an area specifically for the collection of seed. By 1920 the seed field was extensive enough to support the establishment of the Benvenuto Seed Company and a catalogue of seeds available was produced. Seed was collected and packaged for sale from a wide variety of plants. This tradition of harvesting the home-grown seed continued until the development of homes with gardens bordering The Butchart Gardens made it difficult. In addition to cross-pollination, which caused a shortage of pure and reliable seed of certain varieties, there were also problems with space for the seed fields. The collection, drying and cleaning of seed to be packaged for sale took staff from the ever increasing number of gardening tasks. Nowadays tested seed is purchased from leading seed producers. The seed is tested for a second time here at the Gardens and packaged by hand by the staff of the Seed and Gift Store.

Mr. and Mrs. Butchart entertaining the Duke and Duchess of Connaught in 1912 on board Mr. Butchart's yacht the Nooya

Jennie and Robert Butchart never tired of entertaining their friends in addition to many guests of the City of Victoria and the Province of British Columbia. R.P. went out of his way to point out that the credit for the creation of such beauty was due solely to his wife's efforts and inspiration. However, it was he who was honoured in 1928 when he was named Freeman of the City of Victoria. In expressing his thanks he said, "Mrs. Butchart has looked for years on the Saanich Peninsula as one of the most beautiful places in the world, and we have tried in our modest way to keep it so." Happily, Jennie was presented with her own award as Victoria's Citizen of the Year in 1931.

After a long illness, their son-in-law Harry Ross died in 1930. Three years later his widow married a dashing Russian emigré the family had met in Paris while on a trip to Europe. Jennie's marriage to Prince André Chirinsky-Chikhmatoff took place in Toronto. She returned with her husband to make their home on the west coast.

The key to the city

In June of 1928 Mr. and Mrs. Butchart were invited to the City Hall of Victoria for a presentation. R.P. Butchart was made Freeman of the City of Victoria. This high civic honour was accompanied by an illuminated address and a silver chest containing a key to the city. He was only the second citizen to achieve this honour, the other being His Excellency the Governor-General of Canada, Viscount Lord Willingdon who received this award the previous year.

Jennie Butchart was given special recognition in 1931 when she was named Greater Victoria's 'Best Citizen' at a banquet held in the Empress Hotel by the Native Sons and Native Daughters of British Columbia.

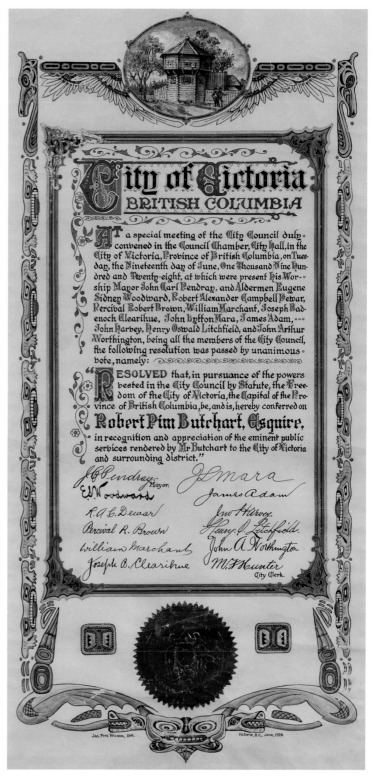

Freeman of the city proclamation

Mr. and Mrs. Butchart circa 1935

Photo by H.U. Knight

Ian Ross with his grandmother Jennie
and cousins Terese and Terry

Ian Ross with his mother Jennie

The Butchart daughters, Jennie and Mary, lived in the city of Victoria. Jennie married Harry Ross who worked at the Tod Inlet factory. Their home was in the Municipality of Oak Bay where their son Ian was born in 1918. Her sister Mary lived with her husband Will Todd and their three children in Victoria. The Todd family had substantial interests in the west coast salmon canneries and lumber. The four grandchildren spent many happy weekends and holidays at Benvenuto where their grandparents, especially Grandma Jennie, doted on them.

Ian Ross at age 21 when he was gifted The Gardens

As the years passed R.P. was weakened by ill-health and he found it necessary to move with Jennie into Victoria. Plans were made for the future of their gardens and in 1939 the Butcharts made a gift of Benvenuto to one of their grandsons, Ian Ross, on his 21st birthday.

Ian Ross was attending McGill University in Montreal at the time and the clouds of World War II were gathering on the horizon. On graduating he had decided to attend law school in Toronto. However, world events prevented this. At the start of the war he enlisted in the Royal Canadian Navy, was commissioned and posted to Halifax on the east coast. For the next six years he was unable to oversee the care and maintenance of the gardens or the forest surrounding them. In an effort to prevent deterioration of the estate a proposal was put forward by the family's lawyer.

It was suggested that the City of Victoria and its neighbouring municipalities might assume the responsibility for the upkeep of the garden and profit from any income from visitors under the terms of a ten year lease. The plan was greeted with enthusiasm but thwarted by a municipal bylaw. Land could not be accepted for commercial use, only as public parkland.

As Jennie and R.P. always disapproved of charging an admission to visit their gardens, there was an impasse in the initial efforts to defray the running costs by introducing one. Consequently under the straitened circumstances of the war years, The Butchart Gardens was not as well-maintained as had been previously.

Douglas Hall
Montreal
Dec 19th.

Dearest Granny and Grandpa:

Mummy has just written telling of your wonderful gift and arrangements for my far distant future. It seems like a Fairy tale come true. How am I to thank you for your most generous kindness. I shall endeavour to live up to your trust and try to shape my life along the lines that will fit me best to follow your splendid example in all things. I wish I could be with you at Christmas to better express my feelings of sincere appreciation, gratefulness and love, for the happiness you are now giving and have always given me.

Although far away in person — I shall be near in spirit and my thoughts will be with you at Christmas. I send my best wishes for a merry Christmas and a very happy New Year to you, Granny and Grandpa. God bless you both.

ever lovingly
Ian.

Ian and Ann-Lee Ross on their wedding day

While in the service, Ian married Ann-Lee Brady in 1941. A vivacious young woman who had a great love of the stage and music, Ann-Lee was from Chicago and first met Ian, his mother and grandparents on board the ocean liner Franconia in 1935 while travelling with her mother. Their son Christopher was born in 1944 and daughter Robin in 1946. After 1945, Ian Ross returned from his wartime duties to continue his studies in law at the University of Toronto. Approximately one year into these studies he was faced with an important decision. His gardens out on the west coast were fast becoming in need of attention following the wartime years of neglect.

Photo by George N.Y. Simpson

Robin and Christopher selling ice cream bars
with family dog Gilda

Investments would have to be made, both physical and financial. He could either pursue his law studies or turn his efforts to the enormous task of making his grandmother's garden into a self-sustaining attraction by transforming it into a major tourist destination. Fortunately for the tourism industry of Victoria, British Columbia and Canada, he chose the latter. The task for Ian and Ann-Lee was indeed a massive one and they accomplished it in a unique and practical manner!

Ian Ross with his daughter Robin and son
Christopher in the background

Ian and Ann-Lee Ross circa 1968

For more than 50 years Ian Ross was completely involved with every facet of the operation of his gardens. He could be seen in the early nineteen fifties operating the tractor, building dams, planting annual bedding plants and all the other tasks necessary to restore and polish the jewel of a garden that his grandmother had created and left to his care. Meanwhile Ann-Lee converted the conservatory area of the residence into the Benvenuto Teahouse introducing the tradition of afternoon tea in the residence at The Butchart Gardens which is carried on to this day. Their energetic and creative responses to the challenges they faced helped to gather around them a large and loyal staff of plumbers, electricians and carpenters in addition to a team of imaginative and hardworking gardeners.

Securing a consistent and reliable flow of visitors to Victoria and Vancouver Island was essential to the success of the Gardens. With this in mind, Ian Ross became directly involved with the Victoria Publicity Bureau. This organisation had been started in the 1920's by George Warren who became famous in the Pacific Northwest for introducing the slogan "Follow the Birds to Vancouver Island".

Ian Ross, on left, helping load a truck with soil

He became a legend for erecting a billboard on the Vancouver waterfront close to where the Canadian Pacific boat sailed from the mainland to British Columbia's capital city Victoria on Vancouver Island. The billboard bore his slogan followed by the words "More sunshine, less rain!" which, although true, did not endear him to the Vancouver Chamber of Commerce. The billboard was later removed. Ian Ross became enthusiastically aware of the value of this form of publicity and posted The Butchart Gardens' billboards at several locations on the main highway, down the west coast of the United States as far south as San Diego and in Canada as far east as Alberta on the Trans Canada highway. This Butchart Gardens' advertising strategy led to a huge increase in the number of visitors to Victoria, Vancouver Island and the province of British Columbia.

The Butchart Gardens has always been open to visitors every day of the year. In the early years once the spring show of daffodils, hyacinths and blossoming trees began, an admission charge was collected at the gate. This entrance fee was in operation until it was time to plant the bulbs in late October when it was removed.

Photo by George N.Y. Simpson

Symphony concerts were held on the residence main lawn many
summers between 1953 and 1967

In 1953 the Rosses introduced entertainment into the gardens with a
series of concerts by the Victoria Symphony Orchestra. These concerts
proved to be tremendously popular and showcased several artists destined
to become world famous opera divas, Teresa Stratas and Grace Bumbury
among them.

In 1954, in celebration of the gardens 50th anniversary, the night illuminations were introduced increasing the summer spectacle. The underground wiring for this lighting system made it the most extensive of its kind in North America for its time.

Above: The residence at night. The Italian Garden could be viewed from the bowling alley, swimming pool, billiard room, and breakfast room.
Right: The Sunken Garden at dusk

Puppet shows in front of the residence

In order that visitors would wait until it was dark enough to enjoy the gardens by night, regular evening stage musical shows were presented. The Sunset Shows as they were called, involved local professional artists and musicians in addition to spectacularly colourful sets and costumes which served to enhance the floral setting. The Ross family were totally involved with these shows. Ian and Ann-Lee Ross were producers and both their children were on the stage. Christopher was a wonderfully gifted dancer with a great interest in Broadway musicals. He directed and performed in the shows for many years. His sister Robin was a popular folk singer who also appeared in many of the choreographed numbers.

The stage show "Just for Fun"

The Ross Fountain

At the southern end of the Sunken Garden there is a small water-filled quarry. This was the site of a good deposit of limestone which was first worked in 1869 by a Scotsman from the Orkney Isles, John Greig. He was a lime-burner. The limestone which he crushed and burned in his kiln was used for whitewash, agricultural lime and cement. His two sons carried on the business until it was purchased by the Saanich Lime Company. The quarry was then acquired by the Vancouver Portland Cement Company in 1904 under the direction of Robert Pim Butchart.

In 1964 Ian Ross decided to celebrate the 60th year of the Gardens by creating a fountain display in the quarry. The project took more than a year to complete with most of the work going on behind a tall fence which separated it from the Sunken Garden. Ian Ross searched for information on other fountains that he had seen while travelling and found it hard to come by. He finally resolved to put together a series of moving jets mounted on a floating platform and connected to powerful pumps. In this project he had great technical assistance from the plumber Adrian Butler and the electrician Vic Dawson.

Finally the fence was removed and the Ross Fountain became part of The Butchart Gardens! With 200 nozzles projecting 500 gallons of water over 70 feet into the air, the pumphouse required two 10 horsepower pump engines. The platform on the surface of the quarry lake holding this array of oscillating nozzles was skillfully hidden by a curtain of fine spray. Powerful floodlights shone up through the mist to illuminate the waving jets of water on summer evenings. With the water and lights being put through an apparently random and endless series of variations the effect was mesmerising. Since its inauguration, the Ross Fountain has been changed little, although the original wooden raft on which it floated has been replaced by a concrete and steel foundation which is adjustable. This base allows for it to be lowered beneath the water surface in winter to avoid freezing damage to the the fine spray jets. A series of five powerful single-jet fountains take the place of the Ross Fountain during the Christmas lighting and the winter months.

Photo by Marlene Dayman

Christopher Ross

Fireworks were added to the entertainment programme on weekends in 1978. Hugely popular and dynamic performances set to music, were created, choreographed and fired by Christopher Ross. These spectacular shows are designed traditionally with set pieces and tableaux synchronised with the music to present a theatrical performance of fire. The location of the pyrotechnics is difficult to improve upon. Using the surface of the reservoir for moving floating set pieces and the wooded hillside across the inlet as a backdrop, the magic of the setting is brightly illuminated by the explosions of rockets and mortars against the night sky.

Ian Ross upon receiving the Order of British Columbia in 1990

Official recognition of R. Ian Ross for his life's work of developing a world class attraction for garden enthusiasts from around the world came in 1990. The Province of British Columbia presented him with the Order of B.C. in the Legislative Chamber of the Provincial Parliament Buildings. During the ceremony Mr. Ross was acknowledged for his inspirational beautification of the Gardens since he assumed active management in 1946. Through his efforts, it was noted, "The Butchart Gardens has, in every respect, become world famous and a delight and inspiration to all British Columbians, Canadians and visitors from many countries of the world."

It was noted that during Expo '67 more than thirty Heads of State were guided and entertained by Mr. and Mrs. Ross and that this generosity was repeated during Expo '86.

In 1992 Ian Ross was invited to Rideau Hall in Ottawa for his investiture as a Member of the Order of Canada. On this occasion it was recorded that he had "brought pleasure and enchantment to millions of visitors for many years, thanks to his dedicated stewardship."

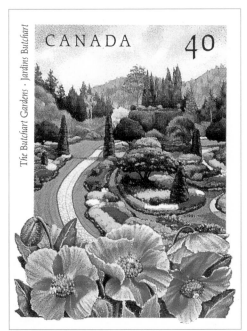

From the Canada Post Great Public Gardens of Canada series

On two occasions The Butchart Gardens has been selected to appear on special Canada Post stamp issues; the first was in May of 1991 as one of a special printing of five "Great Public Gardens of Canada", and then again as part of a "Tourist Attractions of Canada" issue.

In 2005, the Canadian government designated The Butchart Gardens a National Historic Site of Canada recognizing the vision of Jennie Butchart and The Gardens roll in Canadian gardening history.

The Butchart Gardens coat of arms

In November of 1994 the Chief Herald of Canada presented the newly created coat of arms for The Butchart Gardens in celebration of its 90th Anniversary. This coat of arms is a grant of honour from the Crown. Significant features of the Gardens are represented. The rose and the blue poppy are shown on the shield together with the stone steps representing the quarry that is now the Sunken Garden. The tree on the helmet is an arbutus and the wild boars on each side are versions of Tacca the bronze boar from the Piazza. 'Benvenuto' refers not only to the name of the Butchart family estate at Tod Inlet but also to their continuing welcome to visitors from around the globe.

The Sunken Garden during the Christmas Lighting season

Tacca in a festive mood

The outdoor skating rink

From December 1st until Twelfth Night on January 6th, thousands of lights twinkle and glow throughout the gardens. Started in 1987, the display is so large that a lighting crew is busy for a full two months installing it and the massive amount of festive decorations that accompanies it. The installation of the outdoor skating rink provides an opportunity for visitors young and old to enjoy the ice throughout the festive season. Each evening a brass band and carollers perform in the cold night air and hot chocolate and other Christmas treats are near at hand from the cosy Coffee Shop. More formal dining is offered in the Dining Room of the Butchart home in a thoroughly Christmas atmosphere. Over the years Christmas at The Butchart Gardens has become a tradition for thousands of families in the Pacific Northwest.

Eight maids a-milking

Left: The Star Pond

Below: Five Gold Rings glow upon
the Sunken Garden lake

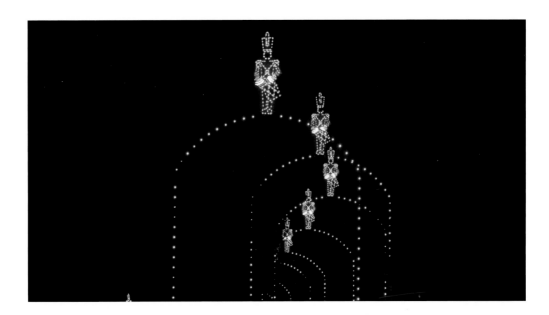

Right: Twelve drummers drumming

Below: Trees above the concert lawn wrapped in lights

41

the Sunken Garden

The nude girl statue

The statue of the Nude Girl is cast in polystone, a material made from Portland cement. The artist is Ed Apt who studied under Elek Imredy - sculptor of the statue of the Girl in a Wetsuit on the seawall in Stanley Park in Vancouver.

A rhododendron grove in the Sunken Garden

Giant poplar trees planted over 90 years ago to hide the cement plant from view

the Italian Garden

This garden was a tennis court before its transformation in 1926. The inspiration for its creation seems to have arisen during a discussion between R.P. Butchart and his guest, Sir Henry Thornton, the head of the Canadian National Railway. With tennis as a pastime apparently losing its attraction a garden was to be planned. At Sir Henry's suggestion an "Italian Garden" was proposed.

A rough design was scribbled on a napkin showing rectangular and symmetrical beds in a paved courtyard and it was given to Samuel MacLure, the prominent Victoria architect who formally designed the garden.

the Star Pond

First built as a duck pond this whitewashed pool and its surrounding plantings were originally designed by Butler Sturtevant of Seattle at the same time as the Rose Garden. The Duck House was created for the pond by Samuel MacLure in 1928. Originally there was an arched circular hedge of cryptomeria japonica around the circumference where the fence now stands. This magnificent planting perished in an incredibly harsh drop in temperature in 1951. There is no recorded significance to the twelve points of the star.

the Japanese Garden

The tranquil Japanese Garden is traversed by a stream and a series of small ponds. There is a fine collection of Japanese maples. In autumn this garden, so green and shaded through the summer, is ablaze with crimson, gold and russet as the leaves on these maples get ready to fall. Many of the ornaments, lanterns, bridges and fountains, returned with Mr. and Mrs. Butchart from their travels to Japan and the Far East.

the Rose Garden

Above: A gated archway leads from the restaurant to the Rose Garden
Right: Looking from the Rose Garden toward the Star Pond

The Rose Garden was developed and planted in 1929 from a plan prepared by Butler S. Sturtevant, a landscape architect from Seattle, Washington. Its creation followed a winter of heavy work leveling the site for the garden. The area (which was once the vegetable garden for the Butcharts) lay on the slope from the trees of the orchard at the side of what is now the Concert Lawn. The Rose Garden was planned at the same time as the Star Pond with its duck house and fountains. The garden contains some 6600 rose plants and in the early part of the season in June a colourful backdrop to the budding roses is supplied by the lofty spires of delphiniums in all shades of blue. Owing to the benevolent climate of southern Vancouver Island the Rose Garden has plants in bloom well into October.

the Private Garden

Mrs. Butchart's Private Garden was designed by Samuel MacLure and built in 1922 to her specifications and to this day is maintained as it was during her lifetime. It is the only area of the Gardens that has never been open to the public. The gracious teahouse is often furnished with items of memorabilia from the family - a fishing rod, gardening hat and such.

Robert Pim Butchart had a lifelong interest in cage-birds and ornamental fowl. A sizeable aviary was constructed on the site of what is now the Begonia Bower.

Tacca, the Butchart boar

The Fountain of the Three Sturgeons and the bronze casting of the wild boar are both from Florence, Italy. They were purchased by Ian and Ann-Lee Ross in 1973. The fountain is a casting made from a much smaller fountain created by Professor Sirio Tofanari in 1958. Other works by this distinguished animalist sculptor include the little donkey and the foal that stand close by the statue of the wild boar on the Piazza in front of the Butchart Residence. The boar is a rare bronze copy of a casting of the marble displayed in the Uffizi Gallery in Florence. This bronze is known affectionately as "Tacca", in honour of Pietro Tacca, the artist who created the statue in 1620. His snout is finely burnished by thousands of visitors who give it an affectionate rub for good luck. Tacca is dedicated to all the children and animals who visit The Butchart Gardens.

The Showhouse provides bloom year round

The Sunken Garden main view seen through the windows of the tea house

During the early months of the year, the gardens at rest are still an amazing sight. Indoor displays such as the Historical Display in the former Butchart residence and Spring Prelude in the Blue Poppy Restaurant are added attractions to visits prior to spring.

Spring Prelude

From mid January through mid March each year, Spring Prelude is planted indoors on the floor of the Blue Poppy Restaurant

Historical Display

At the same time as the Spring Prelude indoor garden, the Butchart Residence houses an historical display. The story of the cement company at Tod Inlet and the development of The Butchart Gardens since 1904 is traced in a display of memorabilia, correspondence and selected pieces of original furniture from the family.

The Billiard Room

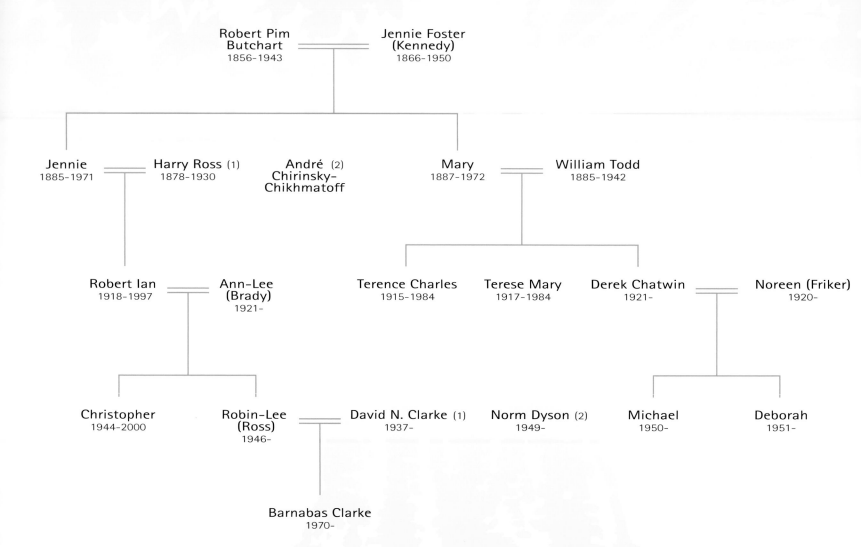

Robert Pim
Butchart
1856–1943
═══════
Jennie Foster
(Kennedy)
1866–1950

Jennie
1885–1971
───── Harry Ross (1)
1878–1930
André (2)
Chirinsky–
Chikhmatoff
Mary
1887–1972
───── William Todd
1885–1942

Robert Ian
1918–1997
───── Ann-Lee
(Brady)
1921–
Terence Charles
1915–1984
Terese Mary
1917–1984
Derek Chatwin
1921–
───── Noreen (Friker)
1920–

Christopher
1944–2000
Robin-Lee
(Ross)
1946–
───── David N. Clarke (1)
1937–
Norm Dyson (2)
1949–
Michael
1950–
Deborah
1951–

Barnabas Clarke
1970–

Three generations: left to right Mr. R. P. Butchart, their daughter Jennie,
her son Ian Ross and Mrs. Jennie Butchart

In 2004 The Butchart Gardens celebrated the one hundredth year since Robert Pim and Jennie arrived and gave their garden its modest beginning with a solitary rose bush and a packet of sweet pea seeds. Since the Butcharts themselves, there have been just three of the family, their grandson, Ian Ross and two great-grandchildren, who in turn have had ownership of the polished jewel which is The Butchart Gardens. Christopher Ross had already brought his own flair into the Gardens with his direction of the stage show and the fantastic fireworks before he inherited control of the family estate when his father died in 1997. Tragically, Christopher passed away in 2000 which left the Gardens to his sister, Robin Clarke, who continues the tradition of family management. The next generation is represented by her son, Barnabas, who is becoming more involved with the operation as time goes on.

" A diamond in the rough is nothing compared to a diamond which has been polished in a beautiful setting.

My grandmother, Mrs. R.P. Butchart, found this diamond and my grandfather provided the setting. "

R. Ian Ross
1918 - 1997